Nelson English

Copymaster Resource Book

YELLOW LEVEL

John Jackman   Wendy Wren

Published in 2001 by:
Nelson Thornes Ltd
Delta Place
27 Bath Road
CHELTENHAM
GL53 7TH
United Kingdom

01 02 03 04 05 / 10 9 8 7 6 5 4 3 2 1

A catalogue record for this book is available from the British Library

ISBN 0-17-424809-1

Illustrations by Denise Colby, Carol Daniels, James Field, Andrew Geeson, Sue King, Mike Lacey, Mary Lonsdale, Gilly Marklew, Terry Riley, Liz Sawyer, Andrew Tewson, Mike Walsh
Page make-up by Clive Sutherland

Printed and bound in Croatia by Zrinski

Contents

Introduction

In this **Copymaster Resource Book**, three copymasters are supplied for use with each unit in Yellow Level *Beginning Fiction Skills* and Yellow Level *Beginning Non-fiction Skills*:

- Comprehension copymaster
- Word skills copymaster
- Writing copymaster.

The copymasters are linked to the texts in the pupil's books, and may be used for support, consolidation, differentiation, extension and homework.

Use the unit 'flag' on the side of each copymaster to help you turn quickly to the copymasters that are relevant to your current work. Fiction copymasters are marked with a black flag (unit number in white), non-fiction with a grey flag (unit number in black).

Four further copiable resources are included in this book – **Spelling Lists** for each unit, a **Look-say-cover-write-check Sheet**, a **Pupil Record Sheet** and an **Assessment Paper**.

The **Spelling Lists** together comprise the key words the children need to learn to spell at this age (see National Literacy Strategy Appendix List 1), and are designed to be cut out and taken home by pupils, so that they can practise learning the words at home. A space has been provided on the Unit 5 Non-fiction list for children's addresses to be added.

The **Look-Say-Cover-Write-Check Sheet** is designed so that the teacher can fill in either the current unit's high-frequency words or other words that are appropriate to the ability of the individual child.

The **Pupil Record Sheet** is designed for the recording of individual pupils' progress throughout each year as they work through the units in the two pupil's books. You may choose to use this as the front cover of a storage folder for that child's work. This will enable you to keep together selected samples of work and will conveniently provide you with the necessary profiling evidence to document each child's progress.

The **Assessment Paper** is designed for use at the end of the school year and notes on administering and marking the paper, as well as the answers, can be found in the **Teacher's Guide**.

Spelling Lists – Year 2 term 1

FOR TEST ON 7/11/05

Unit 1

Fiction

but
old
new
took
or

21/11/05

Unit 2

Fiction

push
pull
over
very
water

5/12.

Unit 3

Fiction

after
once
door
first
last

14/11

Unit 1

Non-fiction

put
too
made
make
want

28/11.

Unit 2

Non-fiction

because
were
them
their
with

12/12

Unit 3

Non-fiction

again
next
another
more
many

Tests will take place on a Monday

Nelson
English

Spelling Lists – Year 2 term 2

---

1   Test on 6ᵗʰ Feb

Unit 4

Fiction

much
must
just
take
half

---

3   27/2

Unit 5

Fiction

sister
brother
people
night
time

---

5   13/3

Unit 6

Fiction

eleven
twelve
thirteen
fourteen
fifteen
sixteen
seventeen
eighteen
nineteen
twenty

---

2   Test 13/2

Unit 4

Non-fiction

could
should
would
these
laugh

6/3   4

Unit 5

Non-fiction

live
school
once
ago
today

---

6.   20/3.

Unit 6

Non-fiction

January
February
March
April
May
June
July
August
September
October
November
December

Nelson Thornes Ltd 2001 © John Jackman and Wendy Wren

Look–say–cover–write–check Sheet

Nelson English

	1	2	3	4

Secrets

Choose a word from the box to complete each sentence below.

mum	Rickie	secret	Libby	teacher

1 Jimmy wanted Roman to tell him the _____ .

2 Jimmy waited for _____ after school.

3 _____ had a little snake in his pocket.

4 Libby told Jimmy that their _____ was getting married.

5 When Jimmy heard the secret he told his _____ .

Word Skills Copymaster 1

Yellow: Fiction

Nelson English

name _____ date _____

'ing'

Write what each person is doing.

| crying | sweeping | playing |
| eating | climbing | throwing |

name _____ date _____

Secrets

A Look at the pictures below.

They show what happened when Libby told Jimmy the secret.

The pictures are in the wrong order.

Number the pictures to show the correct order.

B Each strip of words below is half a sentence.

Draw a line to join the two halves of each sentence.

After school, he

begged Libby to tell him the secret.

When Jimmy got to school, he

told his mum the secret.

As soon as Jimmy got home, he

listened outside the classroom door.

Secret Codes

Draw a line to join each code to the person who uses it.

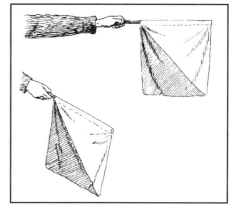

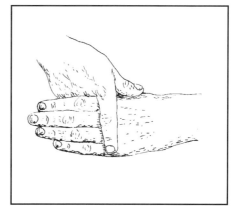

Plurals

The words are going through the plural-making machine.
Write the plurals in the basket underneath.

ball bed boy brother
door code book name school
sister tree cat

Plurals

_____   _____   _____

_____   _____   _____

_____   _____   _____

_____   _____   _____

Addressing Envelopes

Mrs G Potts

5 Lime Street

Willdon

WN6 9YT

A Use the words in the box to finish the instructions for addressing an envelope.

| First | name | Under | address | postcode | Next |

1 _____ , write the person's _____ on

the envelope.

2 _____ , write the _____ .

3 _____ the address, write the _____ .

B Write your own name, address and postcode on this envelope.

_____

_____

_____

_____

unit 2

The Hodgeheg

Look at pages 8 and 9 of your book.
Tick the correct ending for each sentence.

1 At the beginning of the story it was

☐ daytime.   ☐ evening.

2 Max crouched beside

☐ a tall litter bin.   ☐ a street lamp.

3 The humans were

☐ safe.   ☐ in danger.

4 Across the street, Max could see

☐ a litter-bin.   ☐ other humans.

5 Max thought that further along the street there would be

☐ a safe place to cross.   ☐ a street lamp.

6 'Crouched' means

☐ kept near the ground.   ☐ jumped up.

7 'Din' means

☐ silence.   ☐ noise.

8 'Narrow' means

☐ very wide.   ☐ not wide.

9 The raised road where the humans were walking is called

☐ a pavement.   ☐ a bridge.   ☐ a road.

10 The 'noisy monsters' were

☐ hedgehogs.   ☐ cars, motor-bikes, buses and lorries.

☐ humans.

name _____   date _____

'ow' and 'ou'

unit
2

A Read and copy these words.

how   loud   now   proud   flower

B Choose a word from the box to match each picture.

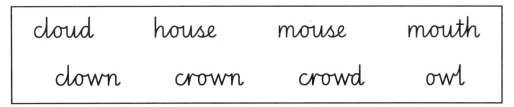

| cloud | house | mouse | mouth |
| clown | crown | crowd | owl |

1  **2**  **3**  **4**

_____ _____ _____ _____

5  **6**  **7**  **8**

_____ _____ _____ _____

C Answer these riddles.

1 What you do if you are cross. Rhymes with 'brown'. _____

2 To call loudly. Rhymes with 'trout'. _____

3 The opposite of 'up'. Rhymes with 'town'. _____

4 A kangaroo has one. Rhymes with 'couch'. _____

unit 2

Crossing the Road

Look at the picture.

Choose a word from the box to fill each gap in the passage below.

zebra crossing	crossed	car	bicycle
lights	stopped	stepped	road

The hedgehog stood at the edge of the _____, near a

_____ _____. A _____ and a

_____ had _____ at the crossing. Their

_____ were very bright. The hedgehog _____

on to the crossing and _____ the road safely.

Road safety

Look at pages 8 and 9 of your book.
Tick the correct ending for each sentence.

1 The instructions are for

☐ driving a car.

☐ keeping safe in the street.

2 When you walk by a road you should

☐ face the traffic coming towards you.

☐ walk with your back to the traffic.

3 When you want to cross the road you should look for

☐ a kerb.

☐ a zebra crossing.

4 When there is no zebra crossing, you have to look right, left and right again

☐ to see if any of your friends are around.

☐ to make sure there is no traffic coming.

5 You should never walk on the road if there is a pavement because

☐ it is safer on the pavement.

☐ you will wear out the road.

6 When it is dark, you should wear something light in colour or
reflective because

☐ it looks nice.

☐ it helps drivers to see you.

unit
2

'ar'

A Read and copy these words.

bar   park   sharp   part   harm   art

B Choose a word from the box to match each picture.

dart	barn	shark	scarf
marsh	tart	harp	lark

1

2

3

4

_____   _____   _____   _____

5

6

7

8

_____   _____   _____   _____

C Answer these riddles.

1 I travel on the road and rhyme with 'far'. What am I? _____

2 I twinkle and rhyme with 'tar'. What am I? _____

3 I am part of your body and rhyme with 'farm'. What am I?

_____

name _____   date _____

Instructions

1   Sam is holding his sister's hand.
Finish this instruction.

Always hold the hand of _____

when you walk near _____ .

2   Sam is walking nearest the road.
Finish this instruction.

Make sure you walk between _____

and _____ .

3   Sam is carrying the ball in a bag.
Finish this instruction.

If you are carrying a ball, put it in a bag so that

_____ *and cause an accident.*

I wouldn't

A Choose words from the box to complete each sentence.

unit
3

floor	play	mouse	hall	mice	house	outside

1 The cat is sitting _____ the _____ _____.

2 The small door is by the _____ _____.

3 The cat asks the _____ to come out and _____.

B In each question, tick the statement that is true.

1 ☐ The cat wants to play with the mice.
   ☐ The cat wants to catch the mice.

2 ☐ I would come out to play with the cat.
   ☐ I would not come out to play with the cat.

C Each word from the box rhymes with another word from the box.
Write the pairs of rhyming words.

floor	nice	house	play	cat	mice
mouse	wall	fat	hall	door	say

_____ _____   _____ _____

_____ _____   _____ _____

_____ _____   _____ _____

Nelson English

Word Skills Copymaster 3

Yellow: Fiction

name _____ date _____

'ai', 'ay' and 'a-e'

A Read and copy these words.

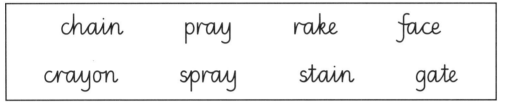

game   say   nail   play   sale   train

unit **3**

B Choose a word from the box to match each picture.

chain	pray	rake	face
crayon	spray	stain	gate

1

2

3

4

_____

_____

_____

_____

5

6

7

8

_____

_____

_____

_____

C Join the dots to make each picture. Write the word.
Write three more words that rhyme with it.

1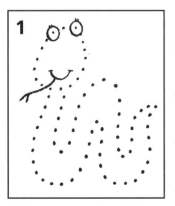

_____

_____

_____

_____

2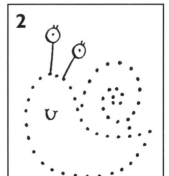

_____

_____

_____

_____

name _____   date _____

Cat and Mouse

A   Choose a word from the box to complete each rhyme

door	wall	mouse	cat

In the hall

There's a _____ .

Near the floor

There's a _____ .

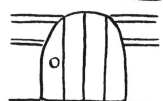

In the house

There's a _____ .

On the mat

There's a _____ .

B   Think of your own word to complete each rhyme.
The pictures will help you.

On the log

There's a _____ .

In the hole

There's a _____ .

name _____   date _____

A hovering Bee

A Look at pages 12 and 13 of your book.
Tick the correct answer to each question.

unit
3

1 What are the instructions for?

☐ catching a bee   ☐ making a bee   ☐ drawing a bee

2 How many instructions are there?

☐ 12   ☐ 13   ☐ 15

3 Why are the instructions numbered?

☐ because it looks nice

☐ because the numbers show the order in which to do things

B Complete each sentence.

1 I would find instruction number _____ the easiest

to do because _____

_____ .

2 I would find instruction number _____ the

hardest to do because _____

_____ .

C Draw circles round the action words in the box.

cut	glue	edge	draw	cone
bend	paper	scrunch	shapes	hang

unit 3

'ee' and 'ea'

A Read and copy these words.

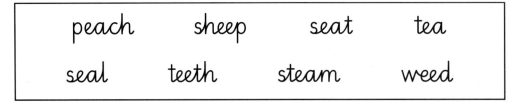

need   deep   sheet   team   leak   heal

B Choose a word from the box to match each picture.

peach	sheep	seat	tea
seal	teeth	steam	weed

1

2

3

4

_____ _____ _____ _____

5

6

7

8

_____ _____ _____ _____

C Write an 'ee' word in each box.

name _____   date _____

Feeding a Dog

1 These pictures show the stages of feeding a dog.
Number the picture to show the correct order.

☐   ☐   ☐   ☐

unit **3**

2 Below are instructions for feeding a dog. They are in the wrong order.
Write each instruction so it starts with an action word that gives an order.
You need to begin each instruction with the word that is underlined.
Remember to use capital letters.

You should <u>put</u> the bowl of food in front of the dog.

☐ _____

You should <u>open</u> the tin of dog food.

☐ _____

You should <u>call</u> your dog to come and eat.

☐ _____

You should <u>use</u> a spoon to put the dog food in the bowl.

☐ _____

3 Write a number in the box in front of each instruction to show the
correct order.

Little Red Riding Hood

Look at pages 18 and 19 of your book.
Tick the correct ending for each sentence.

1 Little Red Riding Hood's mother asked her to

☐ pick some flowers.   ☐ take food to her grandmother.

2 She wanted Little Red Riding Hood to do this because

☐ her grandmother was not well.

☐ her grandmother liked good food.

unit 4

3 As well as a basket of food, Little Red Riding Hood took

☐ some small, pale flowers.

☐ some red flowers.

4 When Little Red Riding Hood set off, I think she was feeling

☐ happy.   ☐ angry.

☐ frightened.

5 When Little Red Riding Hood was alone in the wood, I think she was feeling

☐ happy.   ☐ a little frightened.

☐ very frightened.

6 When Little Red Riding Hood saw 'a dark shape standing in the middle of the path', I think she felt

☐ happy.   ☐ a little frightened.

☐ very frightened.

Nelson Thornes Ltd 2001 © John Jackman and Wendy Wren   May be copied for use in the purchasing school only.

Opposites

A Draw a line to join each word to a word with the opposite meaning.

high	fat
start	huge
tiny	low
thin	weak
strong	outside
light	finish
inside	heavy

unit
4

B Fill in the missing words.
The picture clues will help you.

1 a narrow path

a _____ path

2 a large tree

a _____ tree

3 a hot day

a _____ day

C Add 'un' or 'dis' to each word to make the opposite.

1 ___happy   **2** ___agree   **3** ___safe

4 ___approve   **5** ___honest   **6** ___healthy

Settings

beautiful	horrible	gloomy	colourful
dark	bright	sunny	frightening

A 1 Choose words from the box that tell you what the garden is like. Write them below.

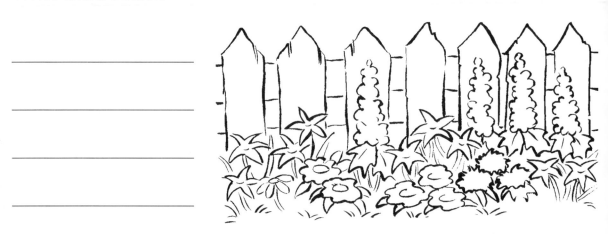

_____

_____

_____

_____

2 Choose words from the box that tell you what the wood is like. Write them below.

_____

_____

_____

_____

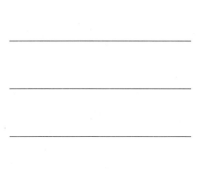

B 1 Use one of the 'garden' words in a sentence about the garden.

_____

2 Use one of the 'wood' words in a sentence about the wood.

_____

unit **4**

A Woodland Dictionary

Tick the correct box to show whether each sentence is true or false.

		True	False
1	An acorn is the nut of an oak tree.	☐	☐
2	Bark is described as a large group of trees.	☐	☐
3	'Forest' is the word before 'hawthorn' in the dictionary.	☐	☐
4	'Trunk' is the word after 'mistletoe' in the dictionary.	☐	☐

5 In the dictionary, you would put:

		True	False
a	'nest' after 'mistletoe'	☐	☐
b	'willow' after 'bark'	☐	☐
c	'ivy' after 'hawthorn'	☐	☐
d	'squirrel' after 'trunk'	☐	☐

unit **4**

Compound Words

A Draw lines to join pairs of words that make compound words.
Write each new word you have made.
The first one has been done to help you.

unit
4

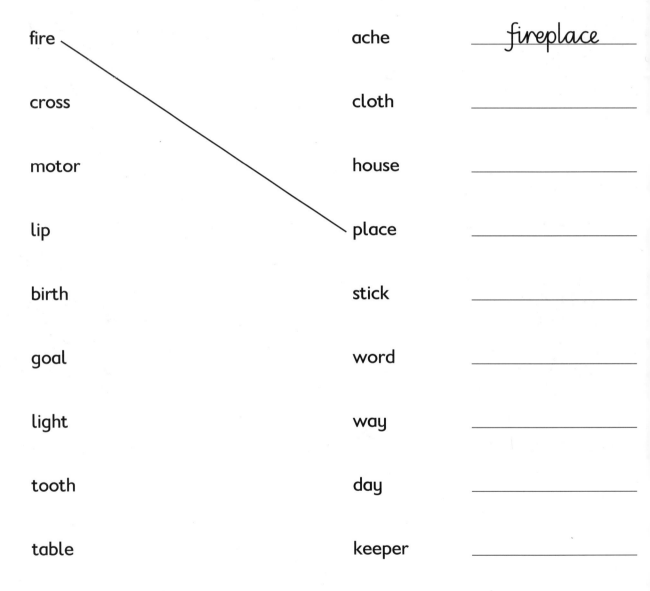

fire	ache	*fireplace*
cross	cloth	_____
motor	house	_____
lip	place	_____
birth	stick	_____
goal	word	_____
light	way	_____
tooth	day	_____
table	keeper	_____

B Add a new word to each word from the box to make a compound word.
The first one has been done to help you.

bed ✓	door	box	foot

bedroom _____ _____ _____

Make a Picture Dictionary

Cut out the pictures and definitions of the trees.
Stick them in alphabetical order to make a picture dictionary.

unit
4

oak
a slow-growing
hardwood tree that
produces acorns

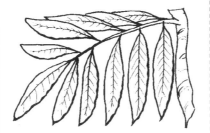

mahogany
a tropical tree with
hard, reddish-brown
wood

yew
a slow-growing
evergreen tree with
poisonous berries

pine
an evergreen tree that
produces cones and
has leaves like needles

birch
a tree that grows very
tall and may have
silvery bark

ash
a tree with silver-grey
bark

willow
a tree which usually
grows near water

elm
a tree with brittle
branches and rough
leaves

sycamore
a fast-growing tree
that has seeds with
wings, called 'keys'

A Dragon in the Classroom

1   The title of the poem is

☐   The Dragon.   ☐   A Dragon in the Classroom.

☐   Our Classroom Dragon.

2   The name of the poet is C_____   T_____.

3   The poem has

☐   2 verses.   ☐   3 verses.   ☐   4 verses.

4   Write down the things the dragon was made from.

b _ _ _   w _ _ _ _ _ –b _ _ _   c _ _ _ _ _ _ _

t _ _ _ _ _   t _ _ _ _ _ _ _ r _ _ _ _ _   t _ _ _

5   Draw lines to join pairs of words that rhyme.

box   holes

rolls   head

said   corridor

jaw   clocks

6   The children

☐   bought the dragon.   ☐   found the dragon.

☐   made the dragon.

7   The dragon surprised the teacher because

☐   it was so big.   ☐   it chased her.   ☐   it was pretty.

unit **5**

Nelson English

Word Skills Copymaster 5

Yellow: Fiction

name _____   date _____

Syllables

1 Look carefully at the passage below.
Draw a circle around the words that have more than one syllable.
The first one has been done to help you.

> If (ever) you should stumble upon a friendly looking dragon, be extremely careful. You cannot be certain whether it is definitely a kind, happy dragon. Unfortunately, some that look cuddly can be surprisingly unfriendly. People have been seen running for their lives, chased by fierce beasts breathing flames and clouds of smoke.

unit
5

2 Choose six of the two-syllable words you circled in question 1.
Write them below, adding a line to divide the syllables.
The first one has been done to help you.

ev/er _____   _____   _____

_____   _____   _____

3 **a** You should have found two three-syllable words.
Write them below, adding lines to divide the syllables.

_____   _____

  b You should have found two four-syllable words.
Write them below, adding lines to divide the syllables.

_____   _____

  c You should have found one five-syllable word.
Write it below, adding a line to divide the syllables.

_____

A Dragon in the Classroom

Draw the dragon you are going to write about.

unit 5

There's a dragon in the classroom:

its body is _____ ,

its head is _____ ,

its eyes are _____ ,

its legs are _____ ,

its claws are _____ ,

its tongue's _____

(_____).

Baby Reptiles

Tick the correct box to show whether each sentence is true or false.

		True	False
1	Reptiles lay eggs.	☐	☐
2	A bird's egg is the same as a reptile's egg.	☐	☐
3	A reptile's egg has a hard shell.	☐	☐
4	A mother rat snake lays her eggs in a nest of leaves or under a rock.	☐	☐
5	A female turtle lays her eggs under a rock.	☐	☐

Tick the correct ending for each sentence.

6 a The shell of an egg

☐ is food for the baby snake.

☐ lets air and moisture through.

b The yolk is

☐ the tiny creature.

☐ food for the young snake.

c A baby rat snake

☐ grows inside the egg.

☐ only grows when it has hatched.

unit
5

name _____ date _____

'er', 'ir' and 'ur'

A Copy these letter patterns.

er

ir

ur

B Write the missing letters in each word.
The picture clues will help you.

1 s k _ _ _ t   **2** t _ _ t l e   **3** n _ _ _ s e   **4** h _ _ b

5 b _ _ _ d   **6** s t _ _ _   **7** b _ _ n   **8** h _ _ _ d

C What am I?

1 You keep money in me.   _____

2 I am the edge of the pavement   _____

3 I am a female child.   _____

unit 5

name _____   date _____

A Flow Diagram

My flow diagram shows the three stages of _____

_____ .

Stage 1

_____

_____

_____

_____

Stage 2

_____

_____

_____

Stage 3

_____

_____

_____

unit
5

The Three Billy Goats Gruff

Look at pages 26 and 27 of your book.
Tick the correct ending for each sentence.

1   The first sentence tells you that the Billy Goats Gruff were

☐ brave.   ☐ hungry.   ☐ frightened.

2   Little Billy Goat Gruff suggested they go across the bridge because

☐ he wanted to meet the troll.   ☐ he liked crossing bridges.

☐ there was plenty of grass in the field across the bridge.

3   It was dangerous to cross the bridge because

☐ the troll lived underneath.   ☐ the bridge was broken.

☐ the bridge was slippery.

4   Little Billy Goat Gruff crossed the bridge first because

☐ he liked to be first.   ☐ he was told to.

☐ he wanted to be eaten.

5   When Little Billy Goat Gruff crossed the bridge

☐ he slipped.   ☐ the others followed him.

☐ the troll jumped out.

6   I think _____ was the greediest

goat because _____

_____ .

7   I think _____ was the most

cowardly goat because _____

_____ .

unit 6

'o-e', 'ow' and 'oa'

A Read and copy these words.

goat   *blow*   *hope*   *soap*   *show*   *woke*

B Choose a word from the box to match each picture.

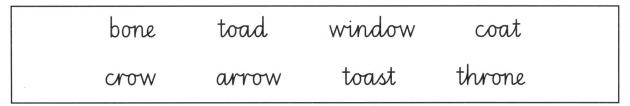

bone   toad   window   coat

crow   arrow   toast   throne

1    **2**    **3**    **4**

_____   _____   _____   _____

5   **6**    **7**    **8**

_____   _____   _____   _____

unit
6

C In each list, write three more words that rhyme and have the same spelling pattern.

boat	snow	nose
_____	_____	_____
_____	_____	_____
_____	_____	_____

name _____   date _____

The Three Billy Goats Gruff

Choose words from the box to describe each of the Billy Goats Gruff.

greedy	small	big	white
not brave	did as he was told		frightened
bossy	middle-sized		cowardly
liked eating grass	brown		timid

unit
6

Little Billy Goat Gruff

_____

_____

_____

_____

Middle Billy Goat Gruff

_____

_____

_____

_____

Big Billy Goat Gruff

_____

Bridges

Look at page 26 of your book.

1 Complete the names of the three types of bridge.

a _____   b _____   s _____

Choose the correct words from the box to fill the gaps.

2 _____ were some of the earliest bridges.

Arch bridges   Beam bridges

3 Modern beam bridges are often made from

_____ .

tree trunks and rocks   steel and concrete

4 A _____ is often used to support the middle of

a long beam bridge.

cable   pier

5 Some of the longest bridges in the world are

_____ .

arch bridges   suspension bridges

6 Look at the index on page 27 of your book.
Tick the page you would look at if you wanted to know about:

   a railway bridges   ☐ pages 17 and 18   ☐ pages 20 to 22

   b cables   ☐ page 14   ☐ page 21

unit
6

name _____   date _____

'igh', 'y' and 'ie'

Choose a word from the box to fill each gap below.

night	try	Dry	ride	stile	time
my	fly	by	bright	kite	bike	cry

1 I will have a _____ on _____ new

_____ this morning.

2 Shall we _____ to _____ our

_____ today?

3 We walked in the _____ sunshine,

then rested _____ a _____.

4 What _____ did you go to bed

last _____?

5 _____ your eyes and don't

_____ .

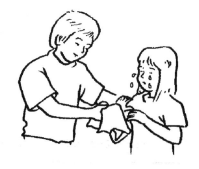

name _____ date _____

Writing an Index

Here are the names of some famous bridges.

Waterloo Bridge	Gard Bridge	Humber Bridge
Sydney Harbour Bridge		Zambezi Bridge
London Bridge	Bridge of Sighs	Tower Bridge

The names have to be put in alphabetical order to make an index.
Write the name of each bridge next to the letter it begins with.

A _____   N _____

B _____   O _____

C _____   P _____

D _____   Q _____

E _____   R _____

F _____   S _____

G _____   T _____

H _____   U _____

I _____   V _____

J _____   W _____

K _____   X _____

L _____   Y _____

M _____   Z _____

unit
6

Copy out your alphabetical list to make an index.

Book Covers

Tick the correct answer to each question.

A Look at the front cover on page 32 of your book.

   1 What is the title? ☐ Mr Timms Catches a Train

       ☐ Mr Timms Learns to Fly   ☐ Mr Timms Goes to Town

   2 Who is the author?

       ☐ Kim Green   ☐ Mr Timms   ☐ Unicorn Books

B Look at the back cover on page 33 of your book.

   1 What is the name of the publisher?

       ☐ Kim Green   ☐ Mr Timms   ☐ Unicorn Books

   2 What is the story about?

       ☐ a train journey   ☐ a car journey   ☐ a plane journey

   3 What did children who had read the book think about it?

       ☐ They disliked it.   ☐ They liked it a little.   ☐ They liked it a lot.

   4 Which of these is the title of another book by Kim Green?

       ☐ Mr Timms Buys a Coat   ☐ Mr Timms Learns to Dance

       ☐ Mr Timms Goes on Holiday

   5 ☐ I like the cover picture   ☐ I do not like the cover picture

       because _____

   6 ☐ I would like to read this book

       ☐ I would not like to read this book

       because _____

unit
7

'oo'

A Look at this letter grid.
Draw circles round the twelve words that have the 'oo' letter pattern.

t	o	o	a	t	g	l
l	s	z	r	o	o	t
d	g	o	f	o	o	l
a	c	o	o	k	d	w
p	o	f	o	i	e	o
b	o	o	t	p	u	o
y	l	o	o	k	h	d

B 1 Write each word from part A under the correct heading.

'oo' sounds like 'oo' in 'book'		'oo' sounds like 'oo' in 'food'	

2 Add to each list two more words with the same 'oo' sound.

A Book Cover

title

illustration

author

✂

Front cover

fold

Back cover

publisher

information about the story

what people thought about the book

titles of other books by the same author

unit **7**

Wheels

Tick the correct ending for each sentence.

A Read the passage about wheels on page 32 of your book.

1 Wheels were invented ☐ 5000 years ago.

☐ 500 years ago.   ☐ more than 5000 years ago.

2 Wheels were first used for

☐ bicycles.   ☐ making pots.   ☐ tractors.

3 Very large tyres are used on

☐ bicycles.   ☐ cars.   ☐ tractors.

B Read the passage on page 33 of your book.

1 The family were going on holiday by

☐ car and train.   ☐ train and plane.   ☐ car and plane.

2 Dad discovered ☐ a puncture.

☐ a missing suitcase.   ☐ he had lost the tickets.

3 It would take a long time to put it right because

☐ there was no spare tyre.   ☐ they had no tools.

☐ the suitcases were on top of the spare tyre.

C Finish these sentences.

1 The passage on page 32 is non-fiction because _____

_____.

2 The passage on page 33 is fiction because _____

_____.

unit 7

'aw', 'au', 'al', 'or' and 'ore'

A Copy these letter patterns.

aw   *au*   *al*   *or*   *ore*

B Add 'aw', 'au', 'al' or 'or' to each word.

1

h _ _ s e

2

h _ _ k

3

s _ _ c e

4

s h _ _ t s

5

s h _ _ l

6

f _ _ k

7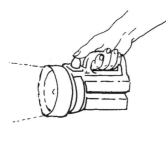

t _ _ c h

8

w _ _ l

9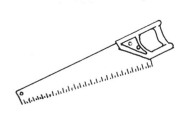

s _ _

C Try to use all these words in one sentence.

cause   *sore*   *paw*   *fall*

_____

unit **7**

A Bicycle

1   Colour this picture of a bicycle.

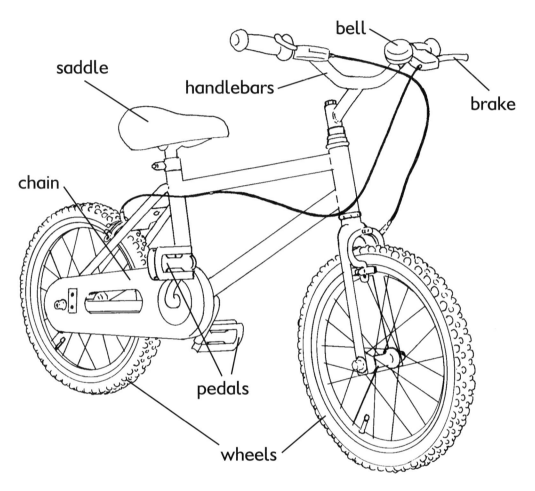

bell

saddle

handlebars

brake

chain

pedals

wheels

2   Use the labels on the drawing to write about the bicycle.
Write about what colour it is and what parts it has.

unit
7

_____

_____

_____

_____

_____

I Wonder Why Dad is so Thoroughly Mad

Look at the poem on page 36 of your book.

1   Look at the **first** verse.
Draw a ring around the two things that happen.

bee in his tea   dye on his tie   slugs in the hall   underwear on the wall

Finish each sentence.

2   Look at the **second** verse.

I think the thing that made Dad most 'mad' was _____
_____ because _____

_____

3   Look at the **third** verse.

The two things that made Dad 'mad' were bread _____
_____ and slugs

_____.

4   Think about the **whole poem**.

If I were Dad I would be most 'mad' about _____
_____ because _____

_____.

5   I think the poem is

☐ funny.   ☐ not funny.

unit
8

name _____   date _____

'ful' and 'ly'

A Finish these word sums.

1 quick + ly = _____   **2** bright + ly = _____

3 loud + ly = _____   **4** hopeful + ly = _____

5 special + ly = _____   **6** helpless + ly = _____

7 silent + ly = _____   **8** free + ly = _____

9 care + ful = _____   **10** hate + ful = _____

11 fear + ful = _____   **12** tear + ful = _____

13 rest + ful = _____   **14** joy + ful = _____

B Use four of the words you made in part A in sentences of your own.

_____

_____

_____

_____

_____

_____

unit
8

name _____   date _____

I Wonder Why Mum is so Thoroughly Glum

I wonder why Mum is so thoroughly glum,

I can't understand it at all,

unless it's a _____ on the carpet _____,

stain	pain
again	rain

or the window I broke with my _____.

wall	ball
hall	tall

Perhaps it's the _____ that I squashed

on the _____,

mug	rug
bug	hug

or the lizard she found in the _____,

view	stew
flew	new

or the unpleasant _____ on her

favourite _____,

guess	dress
press	mess

or her trainers both covered with _____.

too	moo
glue	you

unit 8

People

Look at the passage on pages 36–37 of your book.
Tick the correct ending for each sentence.

1 The title of the passage is

☐ 'Tall and Short'.   ☐ 'Tall People'.   ☐ 'Short and Tall'.

2 The two sub-headings are

☐ 'Very short people' and 'Very tall people'.

☐ 'Tall people' and 'Short people'.

3 The passage is a piece of

☐ fiction, telling a story.   ☐ non-fiction, giving information.

4 Most men grow to a height of

☐ 160 cm to 170 cm.   ☐ 170 cm to 180 cm.   ☐ 247 cm to 272 cm.

5 Most women grow to a height of

☐ 160 cm to 170 cm.   ☐ 170 cm to 180 cm.   ☐ 247 cm to 272 cm.

6 The tallest man in history was

☐ Gul Mohammed.   ☐ Robert Wadlow.   ☐ Zeng Jinlian.

7 The tallest woman in history was

☐ Gul Mohammed.   ☐ Robert Wadlow.   ☐ Zeng Jinlian.

8 The shortest ever adult was

☐ Gul Mohammed.   ☐ Robert Wadlow.   ☐ Zeng Jinlian.

9 Gul Mohammed lived in

☐ the USA.   ☐ China.   ☐ India.

unit
8

Word Skills Copymaster 8

Yellow: Non-fiction

English   name _____   date _____

Comparing words

For each question, write the correct word from the box underneath each picture, then complete the sentence.

1

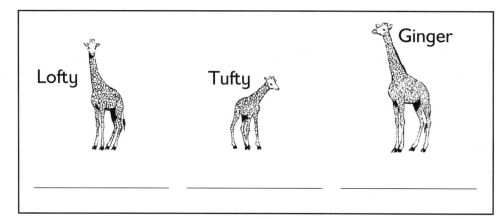

Lofty   Tufty   Ginger

_____   _____   _____

tall
taller
tallest

Ginger is the _____ giraffe.

2

Jumbo   Jimbo   Timbo

_____   _____   _____

big
bigger
biggest

Timbo is _____ than Jimbo.

3

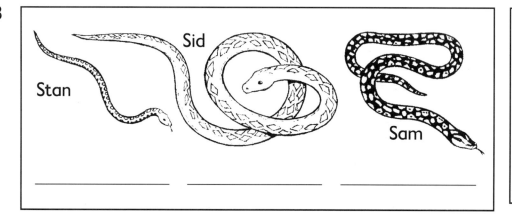

Stan   Sid   Sam

_____   _____   _____

long
longer
longest

Sam is _____ than Stan.

Nelson Thornes Ltd 2001 © John Jackman and Wendy Wren

unit
8

Tall and short People

What can you find out about Gul Mohammed?

Where did Gul live? _____ How tall was Gul? _____

What can you find out about Robert Wadlow?

Where did he live? _____ How tall was he? _____

What was his shoe size? _____

How long were his shoes? _____

What can you find out about Zeng Jinlian?

Where did Zeng live? _____ How tall was Zeng? _____

Use your notes to write sentences about each person.

Robert Wadlow _____

_____

_____

Zeng Jinlian _____

_____

_____

_____

Gul Mohammed _____

_____

unit
8

One Snowy Night

Look at the passage on pages 40 to 42 of your book.
Tick the correct ending for each sentence.

1 The story takes place

☐ in the wood.

☐ in Percy's hut.

☐ in the rabbits' burrow.

2 In the story it is

☐ raining.   ☐ sunny.   ☐ snowing.

3 The first to knock on Percy's door was

☐ a rabbit.   ☐ a squirrel.   ☐ two rabbits.

4 When Percy opened the door the second time, he saw

☐ a rabbit.   ☐ a squirrel.   ☐ two rabbits.

5 When there was a third knock at the door, I think it was

☐ the postman.

☐ a cold, little animal.

☐ the window cleaner.

6 I think Percy is

☐ an unkind person.   ☐ a selfish person.   ☐ a kind person.

unit **9**

'wh' words

Make up five questions about the picture.
Each question should begin with a 'wh' word.

_____

_____

_____

_____

_____

unit
9

name _____   date _____

Setting, plot and characters

Story title _____

Setting
Think about:
• where your story happens
• what time it is
• what the weather is like.

Plot
Think about:
• how your story begins
• what happens in the middle
• how your story ends.

Characters
Think about:
• the names of your characters
• what the characters look like
• what they are like and how they behave.

unit
9

name _____   date _____

Weather report

Look at the passage on pages 40–42 of your book.

A Tick the correct ending for each sentence.

1 The passage is

☐ a report about the weather in Britain.

☐ a story about the weather.

☐ a report about the weather in Scotland.

2 The passage is   ☐ fiction.   ☐ non-fiction.

Complete each sentence.

3 The main heading is_____ .

4 The sub-headings in the report are _____ ,

_____ _____ _____ _____

and _____ .

B Tick the correct ending for each sentence.

1 The clouds and rain are coming from the

☐ West.   ☐ East.   ☐ North.   ☐ South.

2 The weather in Scotland is described as

☐ foggy and warm.   ☐ cool and rainy.   ☐ warm and rainy.

3 In the morning, in Wales and Northern Ireland there may be

☐ snow.   ☐ thunder storms.   ☐ fog.

4 In England, the winds will be especially strong

☐ in the mountains.   ☐ in the morning.   ☐ on the coast.

unit
9

name _____ date _____

Words with similar meanings

A Draw lines to join each word on the left with all the words on the right that have a similar meaning.
The first one has been done to help you.

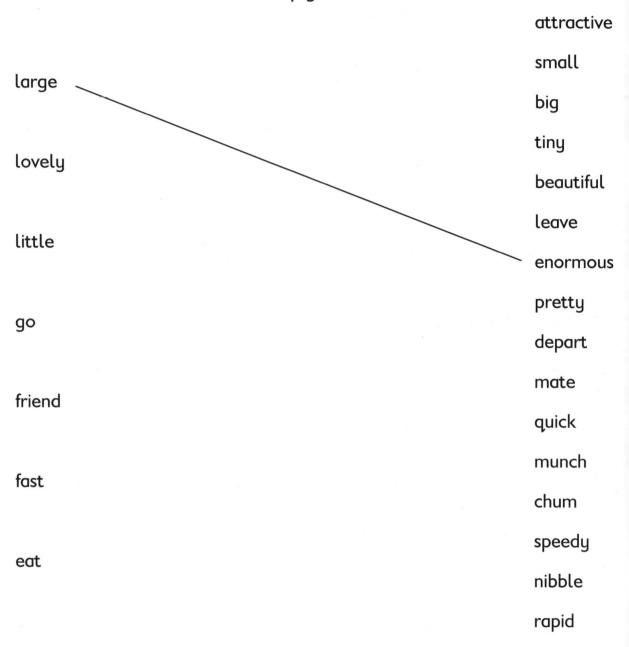

large

lovely

little

go

friend

fast

eat

attractive

small

big

tiny

beautiful

leave

enormous

pretty

depart

mate

quick

munch

chum

speedy

nibble

rapid

B Beside each word, write a word that has a similar meaning.

1 yell _____ 2 rush _____

3 speak _____ 4 giggle _____

unit 9

name _____   date _____

Weather report

Use the map and the notes on pages 40 to 42 of your book to help you complete the sentences in this weather report for Shell Island.

WEATHER REPORT

The weather in the West

In the morning it will be _____ and _____

_____ will fall. It will be _____ .

In the _____ the _____ will break up and

there will be _____ _____ .

In the evening, there will be _____ _____

and it will be _____ _____ .

The weather in the _____

The morning will be _____ _____ and

_____ . There will be a _____ _____

blowing.

By _____ the wind will be _____ and the sky

will be _____ .

In the _____ it will be _____ _____

and there is a possibility of _____ falling.

unit
9

Nelson Thornes Ltd 2001 © John Jackman and Wendy Wren   May be copied for use in the purchasing school only.

Nelson English

YELLOW LEVEL ASSESSMENT PAPER

Rats

Name

Scores

Comprehension Test – Fiction

Comprehension Test – Non-fiction

Writing Test

Total score

Spelling Test – pictorial

Spelling Test – dictation

Comprehension Test
Fiction

Rats!

Once upon a time, in a town called Hamlyn, the people were very unhappy.

They were unhappy because their town was full of rats.

There were rats everywhere. In the daytime the rats ate all the food. They nibbled holes in all the clothes. They frightened the children.

At night, the noise made by the rats kept everyone awake.

Something had to be done!

1 Which words tell you this is the beginning of the story?

_____ ◯

2 What did the rats do in the night?

☐ They ate the food.   ☐ They made holes in the clothes.

☐ They kept everyone awake.   ☐ They frightened the children. ◯

1

Nelson Thornes Ltd 2001 © John Jackman and Wendy Wren

The Mayor of the town was unhappy. He knew that he had to do something but he had no idea what to do.

He asked his wife. She had no idea. He asked his brother. He had no idea. He asked his friends. They had no idea. The people got very angry.

"The Mayor should do something about the rats!" they said. "If he can't get rid of the rats then we should get rid of him!"

The Mayor locked himself in his bedroom and would not come out.

3 Why was the Mayor unhappy?

_____ ⭕

_____

4 What did the Mayor do when the people got angry?

☐ He asked his wife   ☐ He asked his brother
   what to do.   what to do.

☐ He locked himself in   ☐ He asked his friends
   his bedroom.   what to do.   ⭕

2

One day, a strange-looking man came to the town. He was very tall and very thin. Half of his clothes were yellow and the other half were red.

He went to the Mayor's house and banged on the door.

"I can get rid of the rats for you!" he shouted.

The Mayor quickly unlocked his bedroom door, hurried down the stairs and let the stranger in.

"You can get rid of the rats?" he cried.

"Yes," replied the stranger. "If you pay me one hundred pounds, I will get rid of the rats."

"I will pay you a thousand pounds if you get rid of the rats!" said the Mayor.

5 What did the stranger look like?

_____

_____

_____

6 How much did the Mayor promise to pay the stranger?

_____

3

The stranger smiled and stepped out into the street.
He took a small pipe from his pocket and began to play.
As the music floated through the air, the rats appeared!

Brown rats, black rats, small rats, big rats,
thin rats and fat rats came from every part of the town.
The stranger began to walk down the street
towards the hills and the rats followed him.
They seemed to be dancing to the music
as they ran and jumped and hopped
after the stranger.

Soon there were no more rats
in the town. People came out of their
houses smiling and shouting.
"The rats have gone! The rats
have gone!" they cried.

7 Write down two other things the rats did.

(a) ran

(b)

(c) ◯

8 Why were the people smiling and shouting?

◯

4

Nelson Thornes Ltd 2001 © John Jackman and Wendy Wren

The Mayor told the townsfolk to clear out the nests the rats had made. Everyone was so busy that they forgot all about the stranger until he came back to the town to speak to the Mayor.

"Excuse me," he said, tapping the Mayor on the shoulder.

"Yes, yes. What is it? Can't you see I am very busy?" said the Mayor crossly.

"There are no more rats in your town," said the stranger. "I would like my thousand pounds, then I will be on my way."

"A thousand pounds!" bellowed the Mayor. "That was just a joke! We'll give you ten pounds. After all, you didn't have to do very much."

The stranger looked angry. "You'll be sorry," he said. "You haven't seen everything I can do."

"Look, just take your ten pounds and leave," said the Mayor, walking away.

5

9 What did the Mayor tell the townsfolk to do?

_____

_____ ◯

10 What did the stranger come back for?

_____ ◯

11 Do you think the Mayor should have given the stranger a thousand pounds? Why?

_____

_____

_____

_____

_____ ◯

12 What do you think the stranger meant when he said "You'll be sorry"?

_____

_____

_____

_____ ◯

The stranger stepped into the middle of the street. He put the pipe to his lips and began to play.

This time, it was not the rats that came rushing out. It was the children. All the boys and girls who lived in the town ran to follow the stranger. They danced and clapped and skipped to the music as he led them out of the town towards the hills. Nothing the people could say or do could stop the children.

Not all of the children could keep up with the stranger. One little boy had a broken leg. He hobbled on his crutches as far as he could but soon he had to stop. As he watched, all the other children reached the side of a hill, and a strange thing happened. The hill seemed to open up and the stranger and the children disappeared inside, never to be seen again.

13 How do you think the people felt when they saw their children following the stranger?

_____

_____

_____

_____ ◯

14 How do you think the little boy with the broken leg felt when he saw the other children disappearing?

_____

_____

_____

_____ ◯

15 What do you think the townsfolk said to the Mayor after the children had gone?

_____

_____

_____

_____ ◯

8

Comprehension Test
Non-fiction

Rodents

The smallest and the biggest

Rats come from a big family of animals called 'rodents'. Most rodents are quite small.

The smallest, called pygmy mice, live in America. Pygmy mice are only about 5 or 6 centimetres long.

The biggest rodents lived at about the time of the dinosaurs and were the size of a small bear. These were called castoroides.

Pygmy mice

---

1 What family of animals do rats belong to?

_____   ◯

2 Which are the smallest?

☐ pygmy mice ☐ rats ☐ castoroides   ◯

3 Which were the biggest?

☐ pygmy mice ☐ rats ☐ castoroides   ◯

9

What do rodents look like?

Rodents are furry animals and have long and very sharp front teeth for gnawing.

Their teeth never stop growing. They get worn down as the animal chews things.

Some have bushy tails and some have tails without any fur.

4 Why do rodents have sharp front teeth?

_____ ◯

5 What do all rodents have?

☐ brown fur   ☐ sharp front teeth

☐ brown eyes   ☐ bushy tails   ◐

10

Where do rodents live?

Rodents live in all parts of the world, in hot countries and in cold countries. Some live high on mountains and others live in valleys. Some, like the beaver, even have webbed feet to help them to swim.

6 Where do rodents live?

☐ Only in hot countries.   ☐ Only in valleys.

☐ In all parts of the world.   ☐ Only in cold countries.   ◯

7 How do we know beavers spend a lot of time in the water?

_____ ◯

11

Rodents as pets

Guinea pigs and hamsters are rodents and are often kept as pets.

Others, such as rats and mice can be good pets but they can also cause problems for people. Wild rats and mice get into lofts, barns and sheds and steal food or chew things to make nests.

8 Which of these pets are rodents? (You can tick more than one box.)

☐ cats   ☐ hamsters   ☐ dogs   ☐ guinea pigs   ◯

9 Which rodent would you like to keep as a pet? Write a sentence to say why.

_____

_____   ◯

10 How do some rodents cause problems for people?

_____

_____   ◯

Nelson Thornes Ltd 2001 © John Jackman and Wendy Wren

Spelling Test – pictorial

13

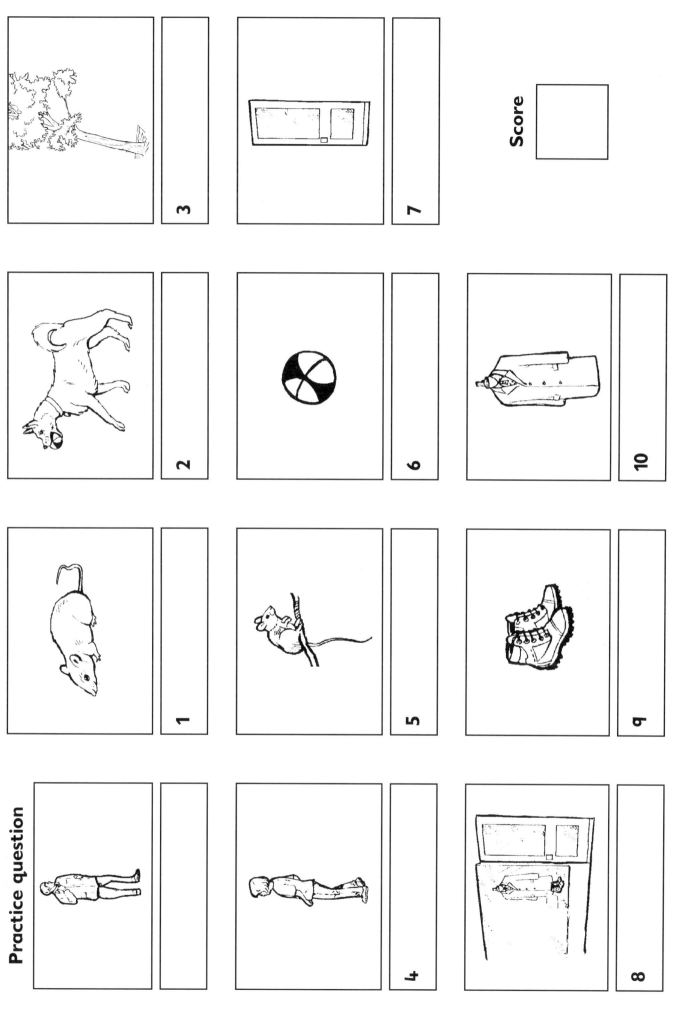

Practice question

3

7

Score

2

6

10

1

5

q

4

8

14

Spelling Test – dictation

Some people are _____ fond of rats, which are

_____ to make _____ pets. But _____

people are frightened by them.

_____ rodents, such as guinea pigs, _____

_____ and _____ are thought to be

_____ and friendly, but just like rats they have sharp

_____ teeth that can _____ a _____

_____ .

If ever you are _____ by an _____ it is

_____ to visit your doctor, _____ some

creatures carry _____ germs. If these get into

_____ blood they can sometimes _____ to

serious _____ .

15

Writing Test

Choose one of the following.

■ Imagine you are one of the children who followed the stranger into the hillside.
Describe what it was like, what you saw and what you did.

■ Imagine you were the little boy who was left behind.
Write a letter to the stranger, asking him to bring back the other children.

Nelson English

Pupil Record Sheet
Yellow Level (Year 2)

Last name _____

First name _____

Key		Comprehension	Spelling	Writing sentences	Writing	Comments
◹ Activity undertaken						
⧅ Activity undertaken and understood						
Unit 1 Secrets	Fiction					
	Non-fiction					
Unit 2 Roads	Fiction					
	Non-fiction					
Unit 3 Animals	Fiction					
	Non-fiction					
Unit 4 Woods	Fiction					
	Non-fiction					
Unit 5 Reptiles	Fiction					
	Non-fiction					
Unit 6 Bridges	Fiction					
	Non-fiction					
Unit 7 Vehicles	Fiction					
	Non-fiction					
Unit 8 People	Fiction					
	Non-fiction					
Unit 9 Weather	Fiction					
	Non-fiction					